# Contents

CW00552419

Working for over **25** YEARS WITH Cambridge Assessment International Education

# Cambridge IGCSE™

# ICT Theory

## Workbook

David Watson

**HODDER EDUCATION**

Although every effort has been made to ensure that website addresses are correct at the time of going to press, Hodder Education cannot be held responsible for the content of any website mentioned in this book. It is sometimes possible to find a relocated web page by typing in the address of the home page for a website in the URL window of your browser.

Hachette UK's policy is to use papers that are natural, renewable and recyclable products and made from wood grown in well-managed forests and other controlled sources. The logging and manufacturing processes are expected to conform to the environmental regulations of the country of origin.

Orders: please contact Hachette UK Distribution, Hely Hutchinson Centre, Milton Road, Didcot, Oxfordshire, OX11 7HH. Telephone: +44 (0)1235 827827. Email education@hachette.co.uk. Lines are open from 9 a.m. to 5 p.m., Monday to Friday. You can also order through our website: www.hoddereducation.com
ISBN 978 1 471890369

© David Watson 2016

First published in 2016
by Hodder Education,
an Hachette UK Company,
Carmelite House
50 Victoria Embankment
London EC4Y 0DZ
www.hoddereducation.com

Impression number  10  9  8  7

Year       2021

All rights reserved. Apart from any use permitted under UK copyright law, no part of this publication may be reproduced or transmitted in any form or by any means, electronic or mechanical, including photocopying and recording, or held within any information storage and retrieval system, without permission in writing from the publisher or under licence from the Copyright Licensing Agency Limited. Further details of such licences (for reprographic reproduction) may be obtained from the Copyright Licensing Agency Limited, Saffron House, 6–10 Kirby Street, London EC1N 8TS.

Cover photo © Oleksiy Mark - Fotolia

Typeset in Frutiger 55 roman, 10/13 pts by Aptara Inc.

Printed in the UK

A catalogue record for this title is available from the British Library

# 1 Types and components of a computer system

1 Name the parts of a computer system shown below:

a ...................................................................................................................................

b ...................................................................................................................................

c ...................................................................................................................................

d ...................................................................................................................................

e ...................................................................................................................................

f ................................................................................................................*[6 marks]*

2 Choose items from the following list to satisfy the definitions below:

compiler     graphics software     source code     video editing software

linker     spreadsheet     database     operating system

utilities     device driver     photo editing software     control and measurement software

| Definition | Item from list |
|---|---|
| Software used to manipulate photographs stored on a computer | .................................................... .................................................... |
| Software which obtains data from sensors allowing computers to monitor and control external activities | .................................................... .................................................... |
| Software used to manipulate and organise numerical data; data is put into a grid of numbered rows and lettered columns | .................................................... .................................................... |
| Software running in the background of a computer which manages most of the basic functions, such as *user interface* and *memory management* | .................................................... .................................................... |
| Software that translates a program written in a high level language into machine code so that it can be directly run on the computer | .................................................... .................................................... |
| Software that takes one or more object files produced by a language translator and combines them into a single program that can be run on a computer | .................................................... .................................................... |
| Software that enables one or more hardware devices to communicate with the computer's operating system | .................................................... .................................................... |

[7 marks]

3 Some of the statements below are **true** and some are **false**. Tick (✔) the appropriate column to indicate which are **true** and which are **false**:

| Statement | True | False |
|---|---|---|
| Streaming videos to mobile phones using 4G networks has faster data transfer rates than using WiFi | | |
| Mainframe computers have smaller internal memories than desktop computers | | |
| Spreadsheets and word processors are examples of *applications software* | | |
| Video cards and sound cards are typical examples of computer software | | |
| Examples of *utilities* include *anti-virus software*, *anti-spyware software* and *screen savers* | | |

[5 marks]

4 Computers can have command line interfaces (CLI) and graphical user interfaces (GUI).

 a Give **two** advantages and **two** disadvantages of both types of user interface:

|  | Advantages | Disadvantages |
|---|---|---|
| CLI | 1 ..........................................................<br><br>..........................................................<br><br>..........................................................<br><br>2 ..........................................................<br><br>..........................................................<br><br>..........................................................<br><br>.......................................................... | 1 ..........................................................<br><br>..........................................................<br><br>..........................................................<br><br>2 ..........................................................<br><br>..........................................................<br><br>..........................................................<br><br>.......................................................... |
| GUI | 1 ..........................................................<br><br>..........................................................<br><br>..........................................................<br><br>2 ..........................................................<br><br>..........................................................<br><br>..........................................................<br><br>.......................................................... | 1 ..........................................................<br><br>..........................................................<br><br>..........................................................<br><br>2 ..........................................................<br><br>..........................................................<br><br>..........................................................<br><br>.......................................................... |

*[8 marks]*

 b Give **one** example of who might use **each** type of user interface.

 CLI ............................................................................................................................................

 ............................................................................................................................................

 GUI ............................................................................................................................................

 ............................................................................................ *[2 marks]*

5   Three types of device are shown below. In **each** case:

    i   name the device.

    ii   give **two** advantages of using the device (compared to the others).

    iii   give **two** disadvantages of using the device (compared to the others).

    iv   give **two** features of each device (which makes it different to the others).

  a

    i   Name ........................................................................................................................

    ii   Advantage 1 ............................................................................................................

       .................................................................................................................................

       Advantage 2 ............................................................................................................

       .................................................................................................................................

    iii   Disadvantage 1 ......................................................................................................

       .................................................................................................................................

       Disadvantage 2 ......................................................................................................

       .................................................................................................................................

    iv   Feature 1 ...............................................................................................................

       .................................................................................................................................

       Feature 2 ...............................................................................................................

       ............................................................................................................... *[6 marks]*

  b

    i   Name ........................................................................................................................

    ii   Advantage 1 ............................................................................................................

       .................................................................................................................................

       Advantage 2 ............................................................................................................

       .................................................................................................................................

    iii   Disadvantage 1 ......................................................................................................

       .................................................................................................................................

       Disadvantage 2 ......................................................................................................

       .................................................................................................................................

    iv   Feature 1 ...............................................................................................................

       .................................................................................................................................

       Feature 2 ...............................................................................................................

       ............................................................................................................... *[6 marks]*

c

  i  Name ................................................................................................

  ii  Advantage 1 .........................................................................................

   .............................................................................................................

   Advantage 2 .........................................................................................

   .............................................................................................................

  iii  Disadvantage 1 .....................................................................................

   .............................................................................................................

   Disadvantage 2 .....................................................................................

   .............................................................................................................

  iv  Feature 1 .............................................................................................

   .............................................................................................................

   Feature 2 .............................................................................................

   .............................................................................. *[6 marks]*

6 Which terms are being described below:

a A type of language translator which uses specific software to help in translation from one human language (e.g. French) into another (e.g. German); makes use of terminology databases and translation memories.

.............................................................................................................

.............................................................................................................

b Technology that allows 3-D images to be produced; makes use of laser light source, light diffraction and light intensity reading; as an image is rotated it will appear to move in the same way as the original in three dimensions.

.............................................................................................................

.............................................................................................................

c The science of making a message unintelligible to a hacker; this method uses light and its physical properties to produce a virtually unbreakable coding system.

.............................................................................................................

.............................................................................................................

d Technology that uses data goggles, sensor suits, data gloves or helmets to get a feeling of reality; it is an artificial environment created by software used in training, fashion, engineering and sport, for example.

.............................................................................................................

.............................................................................................................

e A system that allows images to be projected inside the headset in front of the user's eyes; some systems use infra-red light which allows objects to be seen even at night.

.................................................................................................................................

.................................................................................................................................

f A system that uses fingerprint identification, retina scans and voice recognition as a form of security to uniquely identify a user; dynamic profiling is used so that the system learns about the user each time the biometric features are scanned.

.................................................................................................................................

...........................................................................................................[6 marks]

7 Explain each of the following terms:

a RAM .............................................................................................................................

.................................................................................................................................

.................................................................................................................................

b ROM .............................................................................................................................

.................................................................................................................................

.................................................................................................................................

c BIOS...............................................................................................................................

.................................................................................................................................

.................................................................................................................................

d CMOS ...........................................................................................................................

.................................................................................................................................

.................................................................................................................................

e Mother board................................................................................................................

.................................................................................................................................

................................................................................................... [10 marks]

8 There are many emerging technologies such as: Artificial Intelligence (AI), Quantum Cryptography and Virtual Reality (VR).

Using examples of your choice, describe:

- the operation of the technology
- the use of the technology
- the possible impact of the technology.

(You will be marked on the quality of your response.)

.......................................................................................................................................

.......................................................................................................................................

.......................................................................................................................................

.......................................................................................................................................

.......................................................................................................................................

.......................................................................................................................................

.......................................................................................................................................

.......................................................................................................................................

.......................................................................................................................................

.......................................................................................................................................

.......................................................................................................................................

.......................................................................................................................................

.......................................................................................................................................

.......................................................................................................................................

.......................................................................................................................................

.......................................................................................................................................

.......................................................................................................................................

.......................................................................................................... *[8 marks]*

# (2) Input and output devices

1   Four applications are shown in the table. By using a tick (✔) indicate the most appropriate method of inputting data for each application:

| Application | MICR | Touchscreen | Sensor |
|---|---|---|---|
| Reading the numbers found on a cheque | | | |
| Inputting the temperature directly in an industrial process | | | |
| Selecting a choice on an ATM | | | |
| Inputting moisture levels in a greenhouse directly | | | |

[4 marks]

2   a   What is meant by the two terms 'OCR' and 'OMR'?

   i   OCR ...................................................................................................................

   ..........................................................................................................................

   ..........................................................................................................................

   ii  OMR ...................................................................................................................

   ..........................................................................................................................

   .......................................................................................................... [2 marks]

   b   Compare the relative advantages and disadvantages of using OCR and OMR as a method of inputting data from a paper questionnaire.

| OCR | OMR |
|---|---|
| .................................................. | .................................................. |
| .................................................. | .................................................. |
| .................................................. | .................................................. |
| .................................................. | .................................................. |
| .................................................. | .................................................. |
| .................................................. | .................................................. |
| .................................................. | .................................................. |
| .................................................. | .................................................. |
| .................................................. | .................................................. |
| .................................................. | .................................................. |
| .................................................. | .................................................. |
| .................................................. | .................................................. |

[4 marks]

3 a A supermarket uses barcodes on all its items. When a customer goes to check out, a number of input and output devices may be used.

Name **two** input devices and **two** output devices. Give a different use for each named device.

Input device 1 ................................................................................................................................

Use ................................................................................................................................

................................................................................................................................

Input device 2 ................................................................................................................................

Use ................................................................................................................................

................................................................................................................................

Output device 1 ................................................................................................................................

Use ................................................................................................................................

................................................................................................................................

Output device 2 ................................................................................................................................

Use ................................................................................................................................

................................................................................. *[8 marks]*

b Give two advantages to the supermarket manager and two advantages to customers of using barcodes on all items.

Manager

1 ................................................................................................................................

................................................................................................................................

2 ................................................................................................................................

................................................................................................................................

Customer

1 ................................................................................................................................

................................................................................................................................

2 ................................................................................................................................

................................................................................. *[4 marks]*

4 This barcode is known as a QR code:

a What does 'QR' mean? .................................................................................................[1 mark]

b Give two benefits of using QR codes.

1 ...................................................................................................................................

....................................................................................................................................

2 ...................................................................................................................................

............................................................................................................... [2 marks]

c Explain how a tourist could use QR codes at an airport to help plan their holiday.

....................................................................................................................................

....................................................................................................................................

....................................................................................................................................

....................................................................................................................................

....................................................................................................................................

............................................................................................................... [3 marks]

5 a 3-D printers use various ways to produce solid objects. Explain each of the following terms:

i Additive .................................................................................................................

....................................................................................................................................

....................................................................................................................................

ii Direct 3-D printing .................................................................................................

....................................................................................................................................

....................................................................................................................................

....................................................................................................................................

iii Binder 3-D printing ...................................................................................................

.................................................................................................................................

.................................................................................................................................

................................................................................................ *[3 marks]*

b A car enthusiast has bought a car made in 1921. Unfortunately, none of the parts for the car are still made.

Explain how 3-D technology could be used to create any part for this car.

.................................................................................................................................

.................................................................................................................................

.................................................................................................................................

.................................................................................................................................

.................................................................................................................................

.................................................................................................................................

.................................................................................................................................

................................................................................................ *[3 marks]*

c Describe **three** other uses of 3-D printers.

1 ...........................................................................................................................

.................................................................................................................................

2 ...........................................................................................................................

.................................................................................................................................

3 ...........................................................................................................................

................................................................................................ *[3 marks]*

6 Give one use for each of the following input devices:

| Input device | Application |
|---|---|
| Trackerball | |
| Joystick | |
| Concept keyboard | |
| Remote control | |
| Microphone | |

*[5 marks]*

7 Give **three** examples of devices operated by actuators in control applications.

For each named device, give a use in a control application.

Device 1 ..............................................................................................................................

Use ....................................................................................................................................

...........................................................................................................................................

...........................................................................................................................................

Device 2 ..............................................................................................................................

Use ....................................................................................................................................

...........................................................................................................................................

...........................................................................................................................................

Device 3 ..............................................................................................................................

Use ....................................................................................................................................

...........................................................................................................................................

................................................................................................................. *[6 marks]*

8 a Describe three ways in which photographs can be transferred from a digital camera to a computer.

1 ..............................................................................................................................

...........................................................................................................................................

...........................................................................................................................................

2 ..............................................................................................................................

...........................................................................................................................................

...........................................................................................................................................

3 ..............................................................................................................................

...........................................................................................................................................

................................................................................................................. *[3 marks]*

 Photocopying prohibited

b   Most smart phones also have cameras fitted as a standard feature.

Give two reasons why many people still prefer to use a digital camera rather than take photos using their smart phone.

1   ..............................................................................................................................

..............................................................................................................................

..............................................................................................................................

2   ..............................................................................................................................

..............................................................................................................................

.............................................................................................................. *[2 marks]*

9   a   Most modern televisions and computer screens are LCD and use LED back-lit technology.

Give **three** advantages of using LED back-lit technology rather the older CCFL (fluorescent lamp) technology.

1   ..............................................................................................................................

..............................................................................................................................

..............................................................................................................................

2   ..............................................................................................................................

..............................................................................................................................

..............................................................................................................................

3   ..............................................................................................................................

..............................................................................................................................

.............................................................................................................. *[3 marks]*

b   i   Explain the term 'OLED'.

..............................................................................................................................

..............................................................................................................................

..............................................................................................................*[1 mark]*

ii   Give two benefits of using OLED technology rather than LCD.

1   ..............................................................................................................................

..............................................................................................................................

..............................................................................................................................

2 ...................................................................................................................................

...................................................................................................................................

............................................................................................................. *[2 marks]*

10 Describe suitable different applications that use of the following named sensors:

| Sensor | Application |
|---|---|
| Temperature | .........................................................................................<br>.........................................................................................<br>.........................................................................................<br>......................................................................................... |
| Pressure | .........................................................................................<br>.........................................................................................<br>.........................................................................................<br>......................................................................................... |
| Acoustic/sound | .........................................................................................<br>.........................................................................................<br>.........................................................................................<br>......................................................................................... |
| pH | .........................................................................................<br>.........................................................................................<br>.........................................................................................<br>......................................................................................... |
| Humidity/moisture | .........................................................................................<br>.........................................................................................<br>.........................................................................................<br>......................................................................................... |

*[5 marks]*

11 Direct Data Entry (DDE) is used to input data into a computer, removing the need for manual data entry. Give the most appropriate input device for the following data items:

a  data written in special ink at the bottom of bank cheques.

..............................................................................................................................

b  information on the labels of products (such as a can of soup).

..............................................................................................................................

c  shaded boxes or lozenges on a paper-based questionnaire.

   .................................................................................................................................

d  debit and credit card details input at an ATM.

   ............................................................................................................ [4 marks]

12 Seven statements about input/output devices are given below. By ticking (✔) either the True or False column, indicate which statements are true and which are false.

| Statement | True | False |
|---|---|---|
| Webcams record images before being transmitted | | |
| Light pens only work with CRT monitors | | |
| Graphics tablets allow drawings to be modified prior to input | | |
| Data from microphones can be directly processed by a computer | | |
| Optical mice use light to transmit data directly to the computer | | |
| Ergonomic keyboards are much smaller than standard QWERTY keyboards | | |
| Driving (steering) wheels use sensors to detect left/right movement to give the sensation of steering | | |

[7 marks]

13 Describe **i** the use and **ii** the operation of the following devices:

a  RFID

   i  Use .......................................................................................................................

      .................................................................................................................................

      .................................................................................................................................

   ii  Operation ............................................................................................................

      .................................................................................................................................

      .................................................................................................................................

b  contactless card reader .......................................................................................................

   i  Use .......................................................................................................................

      .................................................................................................................................

      .................................................................................................................................

   ii  Operation ............................................................................................................

      .................................................................................................................................

      ............................................................................................................ [6 marks]

14 3-D printers produce solid objects. When data is sent to a 3-D printer, it goes through a number of stages. The stages are shown below. By writing the numbers 1 to 5, put the following stages in the correct order:

| Description of stage | Order of stage |
|---|---|
| 3-D printer is now set up to allow the solid object to be 'printed' | |
| Finalised drawing is imported into 3-D printing software that prepares data in a format understood by the printer | |
| Object removed from the 3-D printer and any unwanted material is cut or washed away to produce a final solid object | |
| Design is made using CAD software or blueprint downloaded from the internet | |
| Solid object is now built up layer by layer; each layer is 0.1 mm thick and printing can take several hours | |

[5 marks]

15 Complete the table by identifying the most appropriate output device for each use:

| Description of use | Name of device |
|---|---|
| Produce high quality 'one-off' printing, such as a photograph | |
| Produces continuous stationery and multi-part printouts | |
| Produces high quality printing where high volume is also required | |
| Produces very large printouts, such as an A0 drawing | |

[4 marks]

16 A chemical process is being monitored by temperature and pH sensors and by a microprocessor. A heater is used to raise the temperature and a valve is controlled to admit acid whenever the pH rises above 5.0. The following diagram is a schematic of the process. Name each of parts numbered 1 to 6.

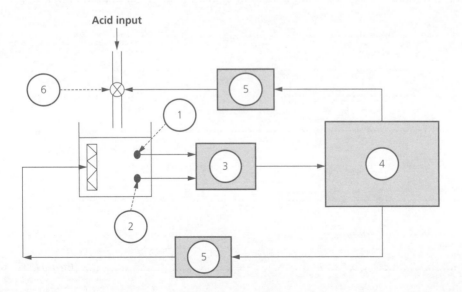

1 ....................................................................................................................................

2 ....................................................................................................................................

3 ....................................................................................................................................

4 ....................................................................................................................................

5 ....................................................................................................................................

6 .......................................................................................................... [*6 marks*]

17 Discuss the relative advantages and disadvantages of using:

- laser printers
- inkjet printers
- dot matrix printers

to produce hard copy output.

....................................................................................................................................

....................................................................................................................................

....................................................................................................................................

....................................................................................................................................

....................................................................................................................................

....................................................................................................................................

....................................................................................................................................

....................................................................................................................................

....................................................................................................................................

....................................................................................................................................

....................................................................................................................................

....................................................................................................................................

....................................................................................................................................

....................................................................................................................................

....................................................................................................................................

.......................................................................................................... [*7 marks*]

# 3 Storage devices and media

1   A bank uses magnetic tapes to update their customer account data at the end of each day. New data is stored on a Transaction File (TF) and this is combined with the Master File (MF) to produce a New Master File (NMF).

The data is stored in account order and part of the TF and MF are shown below:

MF:

| 1 | 2 | 3 | 4 | 6 | 8 | 9 | 11 | 12 |
|---|---|---|---|---|---|---|----|----|

TF:

| 1 | 2 | 4 | 5 | 7 | 8 | 10 | 13 | 14 |
|---|---|---|---|---|---|----|----|----|

a   Show how the data is stored on the merged NMF and indicate which file (TF or MF) the data came from.

NMF:

|  |  |  |  |  |  |  |  |  |  |  |  |  |  |  |  |  |  |
|--|--|--|--|--|--|--|--|--|--|--|--|--|--|--|--|--|--|

TF or MF?

|  |  |  |  |  |  |  |  |  |  |  |  |  |  |  |  |  |  |
|--|--|--|--|--|--|--|--|--|--|--|--|--|--|--|--|--|--|

[4 marks]

b   Indicate which of the following is the largest memory size by ticking (✔) the appropriate box on the right.

| 1 GB |  |
|------|--|
| 1 KB |  |
| 1 TB |  |
| 1 MB |  |

[1 mark]

c   Music files are 4 MB in size. Calculate how many music files could be stored on a memory stick with 4 GB capacity.

...................................................................................................................................................

...................................................................................................................................................

................................................................................................................................ [2 marks]

   Photocopying prohibited

2  Storage media can be classed as magnetic, optical or solid state. Six types of storage media are shown in the table. Tick (✔) the appropriate column in the table to indicate the type of media used in each case.

| Storage device | Magnetic | Optical | Solid state |
|---|---|---|---|
| Hard disk | | | |
| Flash memory card | | | |
| Blu-ray disk | | | |
| CD-ROM | | | |
| Memory stick | | | |
| DVD-RAM | | | |

*[6 marks]*

3  Describe the main differences between Blu-ray discs and DVDs.

..................................................................................................................................

..................................................................................................................................

..................................................................................................................................

..................................................................................................................................

..................................................................................................................................

..................................................................................................................................

..................................................................................................................................

.................................................................................................................. *[4 marks]*

4  a  Discuss the main advantages of using SSD rather than HDD in laptop computers.

..................................................................................................................................

..................................................................................................................................

..................................................................................................................................

..................................................................................................................................

..................................................................................................................................

..................................................................................................................................

..................................................................................................................................

.................................................................................................................. *[4 marks]*

b Name **two** other devices which would make use of SSD and give a reason for your choice; a different reason should be given in each case.

Name 1 ...............................................................................................................................

Reason 1 ...........................................................................................................................

..........................................................................................................................................

Name 2 ...............................................................................................................................

Reason 2 ...........................................................................................................................

............................................................................................................... *[4 marks]*

5 Place each of the following storage and memory devices into their correct category:

| | |
|---|---|
| Blu-ray disc | flash memory/memory stick |
| DVD-RAM | RAM |
| fixed hard disk drive (HDD) | removable hard disk drive (HDD) |
| fixed solid state drive (SSD) | ROM |

| Primary | Secondary | Off-line |
|---|---|---|
| | | |
| | | |
| | | |
| | | |

*[6 marks]*

6 Indicate which type of access each of the following storage media use by ticking (✔) the appropriate box.

| Media | Serial | Direct |
|---|---|---|
| Magnetic tape | | |
| Magnetic disk | | |
| CD-RW | | |

*[3 marks]*

7   A student wrote: 'the future of optical media is one of obsolescence in the next 5 years'.
    Discuss this statement by referring to modern technologies.

    ..................................................................................................................................................

    ..................................................................................................................................................

    ..................................................................................................................................................

    ..................................................................................................................................................

    ..................................................................................................................................................

    ..................................................................................................................................................

    ..................................................................................................................................................

    ..................................................................................................................................................

    ..................................................................................................................................................

    ..................................................................................................................................................

    ....................................................................................................................... *[6 marks]*

# 4 Networks and the effects of using them

1 Ken owns a large shop with a number of computers. He would like each computer to be able to access the internet to enable new orders to be processed and to answer customer queries.

a Identify **three** items of hardware Ken may need to buy to set up a computer network.

1 ................................................................................................................................

................................................................................................................................

2 ................................................................................................................................

................................................................................................................................

3 ................................................................................................................................

.................................................................................................... [3 marks]

b Ken allows his staff to use the computers during their lunchbreaks. Describe **three** ways the staff could make appropriate use of the network.

1 ................................................................................................................................

................................................................................................................................

2 ................................................................................................................................

................................................................................................................................

3 ................................................................................................................................

.................................................................................................... [3 marks]

c It is necessary to back up the shop data, such as customer accounts. Describe a strategy Ken could adopt to back up his data.

................................................................................................................................

................................................................................................................................

................................................................................................................................

................................................................................................................................

................................................................................................................................

................................................................................................................................

.................................................................................................... [3 marks]

d Ken uses passwords to protect against illegal access to customer accounts.

Indicate whether the following passwords are **strong** or **weak**.

| Password | Weak (✔) | Strong (✔) |
|---|---|---|
| Pas5word | | |
| Ken123 | | |
| Ab!*56@@ | | |
| 15April2000 | | |
| TXwm50. | | |

[5 marks]

2 a Explain the following terms:

i LAN ...................................................................................................................

.............................................................................................................................

.............................................................................................................................

ii WAN...................................................................................................................

.............................................................................................................................

.............................................................................................................................

iii WLAN.................................................................................................................

.............................................................................................................................

.................................................................................................................. [6 marks]

b Complete the diagram using the following terms:

   bridge   hub/switch     internet     router     server

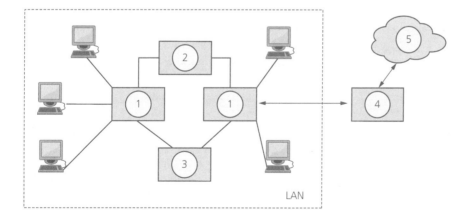

1 ...........................................................................................................................

2 ...........................................................................................................................

3 ...........................................................................................................................

4 ............................................................................................................................

5 .................................................................................................... [5 marks]

c Give **one** advantage and **one** disadvantage of using WLANs rather than LANs.

Advantage ..............................................................................................................

............................................................................................................................

............................................................................................................................

Disadvantage ........................................................................................................

............................................................................................................................

.................................................................................................... [2 marks]

3 a Data is often transmitted using *packets*. Indicate, by using a tick (✔) which of the following information forms part of the packet.

| Item of information | Present |
|---|---|
| Size of the packet (in MB) | |
| Header to identify data packet | |
| Sender's IP address | |
| Identity of each node covering whole route | |
| Identity number of each packet | |

[3 marks]

b Describe what happens when the packets of data arrive together at their destination.

............................................................................................................................

............................................................................................................................

............................................................................................................................

............................................................................................................................

.................................................................................................... [2 marks]

Photocopying prohibited

4   Phablets, laptops and desk top computers can all be used to access the internet.

Discuss the relative advantages and disadvantages of using all three types of device to access information from the internet.

a   Phablets .................................................................................................................................................

.................................................................................................................................................................

.................................................................................................................................................................

.................................................................................................................................................................

.................................................................................................................................................................

.................................................................................................................................................................

b   Laptops .................................................................................................................................................

.................................................................................................................................................................

.................................................................................................................................................................

.................................................................................................................................................................

.................................................................................................................................................................

.................................................................................................................................................................

c   Desk top computers ...........................................................................................................................

.................................................................................................................................................................

.................................................................................................................................................................

.................................................................................................................................................................

.................................................................................................................................................................

.......................................................................................................................... *[9 marks]*

5 Put each of the following statements into the correct column in the table:

- Can be a delay in sending documents if telephone line is busy.

- More likely to be intercepted or read by 'the wrong people'.

- More secure system since documents are password-protected.

- Much easier and quicker to send to multiple recipients.

- Printed documents are usually of a higher quality.

- Received documents can be more easily modified or used in other documents.

- Signatures on received documents can be accepted as legal documents.

| Traditional faxes | Emails |
|---|---|
| | |
| | |
| | |
| | |
| | |
| | |
| | |
| | |
| | |
| | |
| | |

[*7 marks*]

6 Imran is using the internet to research his Geography project. He is using a *search engine* to find suitable information.

Discuss the relative advantages and disadvantages of using the internet to find information compared to the traditional method of using books.

.......................................................................................................................

.......................................................................................................................

.......................................................................................................................

.......................................................................................................................

.......................................................................................................................

.......................................................................................................................

...................................................................................................................................

...................................................................................................................................

................................................................................................................... *[5 marks]*

7   a   Name **three** items of hardware and software needed to carry out video conferencing.

1   ...........................................................................................................................

...........................................................................................................................

2   ...........................................................................................................................

...........................................................................................................................

3   ...........................................................................................................................

...........................................................................................................*[3 marks]*

b   Describe **two** potential issues and **two** clear advantages of using video conferencing
rather than face-to-face meetings.

Potential issues ...........................................................................................................

1   ...........................................................................................................................

...........................................................................................................................

...........................................................................................................................

2   ...........................................................................................................................

...........................................................................................................................

...........................................................................................................................

Advantages ...............................................................................................................

1   ...........................................................................................................................

...........................................................................................................................

...........................................................................................................................

2   ...........................................................................................................................

...........................................................................................................................

................................................................................................... *[4 marks]*

8  Describe the operation of:

a  web conferencing (webinars)...................................................................................................................

.......................................................................................................................................................................

.......................................................................................................................................................................

.......................................................................................................................................................................

.......................................................................................................................................................................

.......................................................................................................................................................................

.......................................................................................................................................................................

.......................................................................................................................................................................

b  phone conferencing...........................................................................................................................

.......................................................................................................................................................................

.......................................................................................................................................................................

.......................................................................................................................................................................

.......................................................................................................................................................................

.......................................................................................................................................................................

.......................................................................................................................................................................

.................................................................................................................................... *[8 marks]*

9  Which terms are being described below:

a  Guidelines to protect individuals, which includes 'data must be accurate' and 'data must be adequate, relevant and not excessive'.

   ..................................................................................................................................

   ..................................................................................................................................

b  Software that can carry out 'heuristic checking' and make use of 'quarantines' to identify and deal with potential computer malware.

   ..................................................................................................................................

   ..................................................................................................................................

c  Additional security item found on ID cards and credit/debit cards to make forgery more difficult; these appear to move or change colour when the card is rotated.

   ..................................................................................................................................

   ..................................................................................................................................

d  Verification that data comes from a secure and trusted source; works with encryption to strengthen internet security (e.g. through biometrics).

   ..................................................................................................................................

   ..................................................................................................................................

e  Wireless communication between devices in close proximity; makes use of 'spread-spectrum frequency hopping'.

   ..................................................................................................................................

   ..................................................................................................................................

f  A transmitter/receiver that allows a device to access a network/internet from any place within 100 metres.

   ..................................................................................................................................

   ..................................................................................................................................

g  When a device wants to communicate, it picks one of 79 Bluetooth channels at random; if the channel is being used, it randomly picks another channel.

   ..................................................................................................................................

   ............................................................................................................ *[7 marks]*

10 'Should the internet be policed?'

Discuss the above statement and draw a reasoned conclusion.

........................................................................................................................................

........................................................................................................................................

........................................................................................................................................

........................................................................................................................................

........................................................................................................................................

........................................................................................................................................

........................................................................................................................................

........................................................................................................................................

........................................................................................................................................

........................................................................................................................................

........................................................................................................................................

........................................................................................................................................

........................................................................................................................................

........................................................................................................................................

........................................................................................................................................

........................................................................................................................................

........................................................................................................................................

........................................................................................................................................

........................................................................................................................................

........................................................................................................................................

*[7 marks]*

# (5) The effects of using ICT

1 A school uses a spreadsheet to keep track of students' test results at the end of each term.

The following section shows part of the end of term 1 results for a group of 100 students:

| | A | B | C | D | E | F | G | | W |
|---|---|---|---|---|---|---|---|---|---|
| 1 | Name | Maths mark (%) | Maths grade | Science mark (%) | Science grade | ICT mark | ICT grade | ... | Class name |
| 2 | R. Khan | 53 | ... | 37 | ... | 50 | ... | ... | ... |
| 3 | N. Chu | 44 | ... | 60 | ... | 61 | ... | ... | ... |
| 4 | F. Kimm | 82 | ... | 65 | ... | 83 | ... | ... | ... |
| ... | ... | ... | ... | ... | ... | ... | ... | ... | ... |
| 102 | Averages | Maths: | 42.5% | Science: | 52.6% | ICT: | 48.9% | ... | (1, 2 or 3) |

a i A mark of 70% or over in any subject is awarded a grade A; a mark of 55% to 69% in any subject is awarded a grade B and a mark of 40% to 54% in any subject is awarded a grade C. Anything below 40% is awarded a grade D.

Write down the formulae that must be in cells C2, C3 and C4 so that the Maths grade for each student can be calculated.

C2 ...........................................................................................................................

...........................................................................................................................

C3 ...........................................................................................................................

...........................................................................................................................

C4 ...........................................................................................................................

........................................................................................................ [3 marks]

ii There are 100 students in this year group. Each student is placed in class 1, class 2 or class 3 according to their combined mark for Maths, Science and ICT. A combined mark of 180 or more places a student in class 1 and a combined mark of 130 to 179 places a student in class 2. All other students are placed in class 3.

Write down the formulae that must be placed in W2, W3 and W4 to calculate which class a student is placed in.

W2...........................................................................................................................

...........................................................................................................................

W3...........................................................................................................................

...........................................................................................................................

W4...........................................................................................................................

........................................................................................................ [3 marks]

b Describe how you could modify the spreadsheet to allow the marks for terms 1, 2 and 3 for each subject to be recorded.

...................................................................................................................................

...................................................................................................................................

...................................................................................................................................

...................................................................................................................................

...................................................................................................................................

...................................................................................................................................

...................................................................................................................................

.......................................................................................................... [3 marks]

c Describe how the spreadsheet could be used to monitor a student's progress; tests in each subject are taken at the end of each term.

...................................................................................................................................

...................................................................................................................................

...................................................................................................................................

...................................................................................................................................

...................................................................................................................................

...................................................................................................................................

...................................................................................................................................

.......................................................................................................... [4 marks]

2 a A manufacturing company has decided to use robots on the production line.

By placing ticks (✔) in the right-hand column of the table, indicate **three** disadvantages to the manufacturers of using robots on the production line.

| Statement | (✔) |
|---|---|
| Redundancy payments to dismissed workers can be expensive | |
| Items produced are not made to a consistent standard | |
| Robots are unable to think for themselves and can repeat errors | |
| Robots don't take any strike action (removal of labour) | |
| Robots are expensive to buy and to maintain | |
| Robots don't make any errors | |
| Remaining workers will need to be paid higher wages | |

[3 marks]

Photocopying prohibited

b Job losses are one of the disadvantages to workers of introducing ICT into the work place.

Describe **three positive** effects of introducing ICT into the workplace.

1 ................................................................................................................................................

................................................................................................................................................

2 ................................................................................................................................................

................................................................................................................................................

3 ................................................................................................................................................

............................................................................................................................... *[3 marks]*

3 Introduction of ICT into the workplace has led to a number of changes to working patterns.

a The normal working hours for an employee at a company is 9am to 5pm Mondays to Fridays.

Describe which working patters are being used for employees A to E according to the table which shows their working hours.

| | | 7am | 8am | 9am | 10am | 11am | 12pm | 1pm | 2pm | 3pm | 4pm | 5pm | 6pm | 7pm | 8pm |
|---|---|---|---|---|---|---|---|---|---|---|---|---|---|---|---|
| Worker A | M | | | | | | | | | | | | | | |
| | Tu | | | | | | | | | | | | | | |
| | W | | | | | | | | | | | | | | |
| | Th | | | | | | | | | | | | | | |
| | F | | | | | | | | | | | | | | |
| Worker B | M | | | | | | | | | | | | | | |
| | Tu | | | | | | | | | | | | | | |
| | W | | | | | | | | | | | | | | |
| | Th | | | | | | | | | | | | | | |
| | F | | | | | | | | | | | | | | |
| Workers C and D | M | | | | | | | | | | | | | | |
| | Tu | | | | | | | | | | | | | | |
| | W | | | | | | | | | | | | | | |
| | Th | | | | | | | | | | | | | | |
| | F | | | | | | | | | | | | | | |
| Worker E | M | | | | | | | | | | | | | | |
| | Tu | | | | | | | | | | | | | | |
| | W | | | | | | | | | | | | | | |
| | Th | | | | | | | | | | | | | | |
| | F | | | | | | | | | | | | | | |

Worker A ........................................................................................................................

................................................................................................................................................

................................................................................................................................................

................................................................................................................................................

................................................................................................................................................

Worker B ......................................................................................................................

..................................................................................................................................

..................................................................................................................................

Workers C and D ...........................................................................................................

..................................................................................................................................

..................................................................................................................................

Worker E .......................................................................................................................

..................................................................................................................................

.................................................................................................................. [4 marks]

b   Describe **three** advantages to the management of the company in allowing different work patterns.

1 ...........................................................................................................................

..................................................................................................................................

..................................................................................................................................

2 ...........................................................................................................................

..................................................................................................................................

..................................................................................................................................

3 ...........................................................................................................................

..................................................................................................................................

.................................................................................................................. [3 marks]

4  a   Name **three** labour-saving devices used in the home which use embedded microprocessors.

1 ...........................................................................................................................

..................................................................................................................................

2 ...........................................................................................................................

..................................................................................................................................

3 ...........................................................................................................................

.................................................................................................................. [3 marks]

b Describe **three** advantages and **three** disadvantages of using labour-saving devices in the home.

Advantages

1 ....................................................................................................................................

....................................................................................................................................

....................................................................................................................................

2 ....................................................................................................................................

....................................................................................................................................

....................................................................................................................................

3 ....................................................................................................................................

....................................................................................................................................

....................................................................................................................................

Disadvantages

1 ....................................................................................................................................

....................................................................................................................................

....................................................................................................................................

2 ....................................................................................................................................

....................................................................................................................................

....................................................................................................................................

3 ....................................................................................................................................

....................................................................................................................................

.................................................................................................................... *[3 marks]*

5  Microprocessors are also used in many other types of device, such as digital cameras.

    a  Name **three** devices (other than labour-saving devices) which use embedded microprocessors.

      1 ................................................................................................................................

      ..................................................................................................................................

      2 ................................................................................................................................

      ..................................................................................................................................

      3 ................................................................................................................................

      .................................................................................................... *[3 marks]*

    b  Give **two** advantages and **two** disadvantages of your named devices in part **a**.

      Advantages

      1 ................................................................................................................................

      ..................................................................................................................................

      ..................................................................................................................................

      2 ................................................................................................................................

      ..................................................................................................................................

      ..................................................................................................................................

      Disadvantages

      1 ................................................................................................................................

      ..................................................................................................................................

      ..................................................................................................................................

      2 ................................................................................................................................

      ..................................................................................................................................

      .................................................................................................... *[4 marks]*

# 6 ICT applications

1 Mike owns a company that wishes to advertise their products and services. He has decided on three possible methods:

- paper-based advertising (flyers, posters and brochures)
- computer-based advertising (using their own website)
- multi-media presentations in local shopping malls.

a Give **three** advantages of using all three methods.

Paper-based advertising

1 ........................................................................................................................................

.............................................................................................................................................

2 ........................................................................................................................................

.............................................................................................................................................

3 ........................................................................................................................................

.............................................................................................................................................

Computer-based advertising

1 ........................................................................................................................................

.............................................................................................................................................

2 ........................................................................................................................................

.............................................................................................................................................

3 ........................................................................................................................................

.............................................................................................................................................

Multi-media advertising in local shopping mall

1 ........................................................................................................................................

.............................................................................................................................................

2 ........................................................................................................................................

.............................................................................................................................................

3 ........................................................................................................................................

.................................................................................................................. [9 marks]

b Cartoons and animation can be used in presentations. Which of the following terms are used to describe the processes used to produce cartoons and animation?

| Term | (✔) |
|---|---|
| Tweening | |
| Morphing | |
| Tags | |
| Rendering | |
| Vector graphics | |
| Formatting | |

[3 marks]

c Mike frequently goes overseas on marketing visits. He uses VoIP to keep in touch with his main office.

i What is meant by VoIP?

..............................................................................................................................................

..............................................................................................................................................

..............................................................................................................................................

..............................................................................................................................................

ii Name **two** devices needed for VoIP.

1 .........................................................................................................................................

2 .........................................................................................................................................

iii Give **one** advantage and **one** disadvantage of using VoIP.

Advantage ...........................................................................................................................

..............................................................................................................................................

Disadvantage......................................................................................................................

.................................................................................................................... [6 marks]

2 Sensors are often used to collect data and then send it to a computer.

a Applications which use sensors are either **measurement** or **control**. In the table, tick (✔) the appropriate column to indicate whether the given application is measurement or control.

| Application | Measurement | Control |
|---|---|---|
| Monitoring the pollution levels in a river | | |
| Burglar alarm system (detection of intruders) | | |
| Maintaining the correct temperature and light conditions in a greenhouse | | |
| Automatic oven cooking food at correct temperature | | |
| Monitoring patient's vital signs in a hospital | | |

[5 marks]

b  Weather stations are examples of measurement applications. Name three pieces of data collected by sensors at a weather station.

1 ....................................................................................................................................................................

2 ....................................................................................................................................................................

3 ................................................................................................................................ [*3 marks*]

c

i  Name the device often needed to enable a computer to process the data coming from a sensor.

......................................................................................................................................................................

......................................................................................................................................................................

ii  Name the device often needed to allow a computer to control output devices such as pumps and switches.

......................................................................................................................................................................

................................................................................................................................ [*2 marks*]

d  Give one suitable application for each of the following sensors. A different application needs to be given in each case.

| Sensor | Application |
|---|---|
| Oxygen/carbon dioxide | |
| Light | |
| Infra-red | |
| Pressure | |
| Acoustic/sound | |
| pH | |

[*6 marks*]

3 A factory makes parts for cars by gluing together aluminium components. When the components arrive at a robot station, the robot automatically deposits glue in the correct places. The panels are then forced together and transferred to an oven for the glue to cure. Components need to be in the oven for 10 minutes at an exact temperature of 295°C.

   a Sensors are used to detect the presence of aluminium components and also to maintain the critical temperature in the oven. Name **two** sensors required for these two tasks:

   i Aluminium panels in correct position.

   .......................................................................................................................................

   .......................................................................................................................................

   ii Maintaining oven temperature.

   .......................................................................................................................................

   .................................................................................................... [2 marks]

   b The sensors send data to a computer. Describe how the sensors and computer are used to

   • ensure robots only apply glue when components have arrived

   • ensure the oven is maintained at its critical temperature.

   .......................................................................................................................................

   .......................................................................................................................................

   .......................................................................................................................................

   .......................................................................................................................................

   .......................................................................................................................................

   .......................................................................................................................................

   .......................................................................................................................................

   .......................................................................................................................................

   .......................................................................................................................................

   .......................................................................................................................................

   .......................................................................................................................................

   .................................................................................................... [6 marks]

4   The instructions to control the movements of a floor turtle are shown below.

| Command | Meaning |
|---|---|
| **FORWARD** *x* | Move *x* cm forward |
| **BACKWARD** *x* | Move *x* cm backward |
| **LEFT** *d* | Turn left through *d* degrees |
| **RIGHT** *d* | Turn right through *d* degrees |
| **REPEAT** *n* | Repeat next set of instructions *n* times |
| **ENDREPEAT** | Finish the repeat loop |
| **PENUP** | Lift the pen up |
| **PENDOWN** | Lower the pen |

The following shape is to be drawn using the above commands (each square is 10 cm by 10 cm).

Complete the set of instructions to draw the shape. Use efficient coding in your answer.

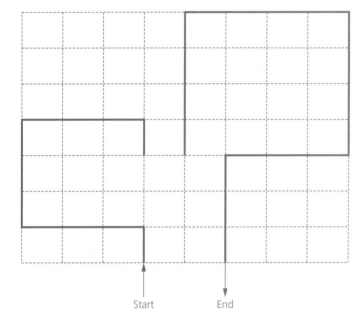

Start    End

Instructions

1   PENDOWN

2   FORWARD 10

3   LEFT 90

4   REPEAT 3

5   ............................

6   ............................

7   ............................

8   ............................

9   ............................

10  ............................

11  ............................

12  ............................

13  ............................

14  ............................

15  ............................

16  ............................

17  ............................

18  ............................

19  ............................

20  ............................

21  ............................

22  ............................

23  ............................

24  ............................

[*6 marks*]

5 A set of traffic lights at a T-junction is to be modelled on a computer.

Before modelling can be carried out there is a need to collect data at the T-junction. This data is then to be input into a computer.

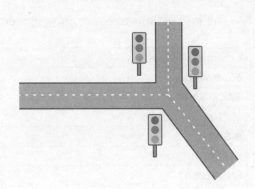

a Describe three pieces of data that would need to be collected for this model.

1 ..................................................................................................................................

..................................................................................................................................

2 ..................................................................................................................................

..................................................................................................................................

3 ..................................................................................................................................

.................................................................................................. . [3 marks]

b Give **three** reasons why modelling is carried out.

1 ..................................................................................................................................

..................................................................................................................................

2 ..................................................................................................................................

..................................................................................................................................

3 ..................................................................................................................................

.................................................................................................. [3 marks]

c The diagram below shows five computer modelling applications and five reasons why modelling is carried out. By drawing arrows, match each application to the best reason why it would be modelled.

| | |
|---|---|
| Car driving simulation | Cost of building the real thing is too expensive |
| Climate change simulation | Some real situations are too dangerous to humans |
| Model the loading on a new bridge | It takes too long to get results back from the real thin |
| Chemical reaction involving toxic chemicals | Almost impossible to do the tasks for real |
| Under-sea exploration | Easier and safer to make changes to a model rather than the real thing |

[5 marks]

6 Robots are used in many factories.

Indicate (✔) which of the following are disadvantages to the management of a company in using robots.

| Reasons | Disadvantage? |
|---|---|
| Robots have difficulty in doing 'one off' tasks | |
| Management can move factories anywhere in the world | |
| Using robots can lead to unemployment | |
| Robots manufacture more items per hour than humans | |
| All items produced using robots are identical | |
| The set up and maintenance of robots is expensive | |

[2 marks]

7 A customer of Hodder Bank would like to check the balance on their bank account.

The customer decides to use the local ATM and inserts their debit card into the ATM:

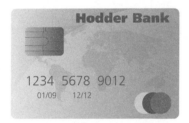

a Describe the computer processing that takes place at the ATM once the customer inserts their card.

..............................................................................................................................

..............................................................................................................................

..............................................................................................................................

..............................................................................................................................

..............................................................................................................................

..............................................................................................................................

..............................................................................................................................

..............................................................................................................................

.......................................................................................................... [4 marks]

b During the customer's request for a current balance, the bank's computer will carry out a number of processes to enable the customer to see their balance.

Describe these processes.

..........................................................................................................................................................

..........................................................................................................................................................

..........................................................................................................................................................

..........................................................................................................................................................

..........................................................................................................................................................

..........................................................................................................................................................

.................................................................................................................................. [3 marks]

8 A customer of Hodder Bank buys an item from a shop using a cheque.

a Name **three** items which are pre-printed in magnetic ink on the cheque.

1 ....................................................................................................................................................

2 ....................................................................................................................................................

3 ...............................................................................................................................[3 marks]

b Describe the stages that are carried out when clearing a cheque.

..........................................................................................................................................................

..........................................................................................................................................................

Photocopying prohibited

.................................................................................................................

.................................................................................................................

.................................................................................................................

.................................................................................................................

.................................................................................................................

.................................................................................................................

.................................................................................................................

.................................................................................................................

.................................................................................................................

................................................................................................. [*5 marks*]

c   Hodder Bank has reviewed the use of magnetic ink and the use of barcodes on their
    cheques to show customer data.

   i   Give **two** reasons why the use of magnetic ink is better than using barcodes on cheques.

      1   ...........................................................................................................

          ...........................................................................................................

      2   ...........................................................................................................

          .....................................................................................................[*2 marks*]

   ii   Describe the different ways magnetic ink and barcodes would be read from the cheque.

      .................................................................................................................

      .................................................................................................................

      .................................................................................................................

      .................................................................................................................

      .................................................................................................................

      .................................................................................................................

      .................................................................................................................

      .................................................................................................................

      ..................................................................................... [*4 marks*]

9  a  Describe **three** types of medical aid which can be produced using a 3-D printer.

1  .............................................................................................................................

...........................................................................................................................

2  .............................................................................................................................

...........................................................................................................................

3  .............................................................................................................................

................................................................................................... [3 marks]

b  Describe why 3-D printers are very useful to surgeons who are about to do constructive surgery.

.................................................................................................................................

.................................................................................................................................

.................................................................................................................................

.................................................................................................................................

.................................................................................................................................

.................................................................................................................................

.................................................................................................................................

.................................................................................................................................

.................................................................................................................................

.................................................................................................................................

.................................................................................................................................

................................................................................................... [5 marks]

10 a  Circle the items below which are components of a typical **Expert System**.

| knowledge base | rules base | encryption system |
|---|---|---|
| explanation system | hyperlinks | inference engine |
| digital to analogue converter | target attribute | analogue to digital converter |

[4 marks]

b Faults in TVs can be identified using Expert System diagnostics.

Describe how an Expert System is used to carry out the diagnostics.

..............................................................................................................................................................

..............................................................................................................................................................

..............................................................................................................................................................

..............................................................................................................................................................

..............................................................................................................................................................

..............................................................................................................................................................

..............................................................................................................................................................

.................................................................................................................................. [*4 marks*]

c Give **three** other uses of Expert Systems.

1 ........................................................................................................................................................

........................................................................................................................................................

2 ........................................................................................................................................................

........................................................................................................................................................

3 ........................................................................................................................................................

.................................................................................................................................. [*3 marks*]

d Describe how a new Expert System could be tested to ensure the results produced were correct when the system was used commercially.

..............................................................................................................................................................

..............................................................................................................................................................

..............................................................................................................................................................

..............................................................................................................................................................

..............................................................................................................................................................

.................................................................................................................................. [*2 marks*]

11 A car with registration number ABC 123 enters a car park. The car park uses ANPR.

  a  What is meant by ANPR?

    ......................................................................................................................................

    ....................................................................................................................[1 mark]

  b  There are nine stages used by ANPR to recognise a car entering and leaving the car park. These nine stages are listed below but are in the wrong order.

    Put the nine stages into the correct order.

    1  Algorithm used to locate and isolate number plate from camera image.

    2  Text string is stored in a database.

    3  Motorist returns to car park and makes payment after inserting his ticket into the machine.

    4  Sensor detects car and sends a signal to the microprocessor to instruct a camera to capture an image of the front of the vehicle.

    5  Motorist drives to exit barrier and ANPR system reads the number plate and checks the database.

    6  Brightness and contrast of number plate adjusted so that the characters can be clearly read.

    7  If the number plate is recognised and payment has been made, the exit barrier is raised.

    8  Once all the checking is done, the car park entrance barrier is raised and the motorist is issued with a ticket showing date and time of entry.

    9  Each character on the number plate is then recognised using OCR; the characters are converted into a text string.

    ......................................................................................................................................

    ......................................................................................................................................

    ......................................................................................................................................

    .................................................................................................................. [9 marks]

12 Give three uses of a **Geographic Information System (GIS).**

    1  ..............................................................................................................................

       ..............................................................................................................................

    2  ..............................................................................................................................

       ..............................................................................................................................

    3  ..............................................................................................................................

       .................................................................................................................. [3 marks]

13 Global Positioning Satellites (GPS) are used to help motorists navigate to a given location.

Indicate (✔) which of the following are **true** and which are **false** statements about GPS.

| Statements | True | False |
|---|---|---|
| The sat nav in the car sends signals to the GPS satellites giving the car's location | | |
| If the maps are not up to date, the driver can be given incorrect instructions | | |
| The satellites move round the Earth keeping track of all the cars | | |
| The sat nav system installed in the car has state-of-the-art timing systems | | |
| The system can estimate the time of arrival of the car at its destination | | |
| Paper maps have been scanned in so that the route shows up on the sat nav screen in the car | | |

[6 marks]

14 Give the meaning of each of the following terms:

a MICR.............................................................................................................................................

.........................................................................................................................................................

b OCR ..............................................................................................................................................

.........................................................................................................................................................

c OMR..............................................................................................................................................

.........................................................................................................................................................

d RFID..............................................................................................................................................

.........................................................................................................................................................

e EPOS.............................................................................................................................................

.........................................................................................................................................................

f MRI................................................................................................................................................

.........................................................................................................................................................

g ATM...............................................................................................................................................

.........................................................................................................................................................

h DAC...............................................................................................................................................

.........................................................................................................................................................

i   SIM .................................................................................................................................

.................................................................................................................................

j   VoIP ...............................................................................................................................

.................................................................................... [10 marks]

15 A cinema has an online booking system.

Describe what happens when a customer visits the cinema's website and chooses to purchase four seats to the see the film *Hachette – the story of a book.*

Include in your description the role of the user and of the website software to ensure purchased tickets can't be double booked.

.................................................................................................................................

.................................................................................................................................

.................................................................................................................................

.................................................................................................................................

.................................................................................................................................

.................................................................................................................................

.................................................................................................................................

.................................................................................................................................

.................................................................................................................................

.................................................................................................................................

.................................................................................................................................

.................................................................................................................................

.................................................................................................................................

.................................................................................................................................

.................................................................................................................................

.................................................................................... [8 marks]

# 7 Systems life cycle

1 Complete the following diagram with the missing stages from the **systems life cycle**.

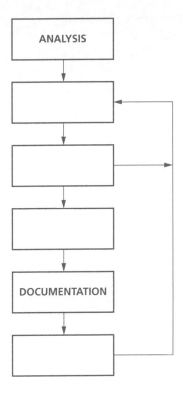

[4 marks]

2 Part of the **analysis** stage involves researching the existing system.

Name **three** methods of gathering information about the existing system. For each named method,

   a give a brief description

   b give **one** advantage

   c give **one** disadvantage.

Method 1 ...........................................................................................................................................................

Description .......................................................................................................................................................

.................................................................................................................................................................................

.................................................................................................................................................................................

Advantage .........................................................................................................................................................

.................................................................................................................................................................................

.................................................................................................................................................................................

Disadvantage ........................................................................................................................

.............................................................................................................................................

.............................................................................................................................................

Method 2 ..............................................................................................................................

.............................................................................................................................................

Description ..........................................................................................................................

.............................................................................................................................................

.............................................................................................................................................

Advantage ...........................................................................................................................

.............................................................................................................................................

.............................................................................................................................................

Disadvantage ......................................................................................................................

.............................................................................................................................................

.............................................................................................................................................

Method 3 ..............................................................................................................................

Description ..........................................................................................................................

.............................................................................................................................................

.............................................................................................................................................

Advantage ...........................................................................................................................

.............................................................................................................................................

.............................................................................................................................................

Disadvantage ......................................................................................................................

.............................................................................................................................................

................................................................................................................... [*12 marks*]

 Photocopying prohibited

3  Two types of diagram used in systems analysis are DFDs and system flowcharts.

Describe the purpose of each type of diagram.

DFD ........................................................................................................................................................

................................................................................................................................................................

................................................................................................................................................................

................................................................................................................................................................

................................................................................................................................................................

System flowchart ................................................................................................................................

................................................................................................................................................................

................................................................................................................................................................

................................................................................................................................................................

................................................................................................................ *[4 marks]*

4  Data capture forms can be paper-based or electronic, online forms.

a  i  Give **five** features you would expect to see in a well-designed paper-based data
capture form.

1 .....................................................................................................................................

.........................................................................................................................................

2 .....................................................................................................................................

.........................................................................................................................................

3 .....................................................................................................................................

.........................................................................................................................................

4 .....................................................................................................................................

.........................................................................................................................................

5 .....................................................................................................................................

.................................................................................................................. *[5 marks]*

ii   Look at the following data capture form designed to collect information about car ownership.

Your name:

................................................................................................................................

Your address:

................................................................................................................................

Reg Number of your car:

................................................................................................................................

Make of car:

................................................................................................................................

Colour of car:

................................................................................................................................

Was it bought new?

................................................................................................................................

When did you buy it (dd/mm/yy):

................................................................................................................................

Design a much improved paper-based form for data capture using some of the features described in part **a i** above.

................................................................................................................................

................................................................................................................................

................................................................................................................................

................................................................................................................................

................................................................................................................................

................................................................................................................................

................................................................................................................................

................................................................................................................................

................................................................................................................................

................................................................................................ *[3 marks]*

b   Computer-based (online) data capture forms are also used.

   i   Give **five** features you would expect to see in a well-designed computer-based data capture form.

   1 ...................................................................................................................................

   ...................................................................................................................................

   2 ...................................................................................................................................

   ...................................................................................................................................

   3 ...................................................................................................................................

   ...................................................................................................................................

   4 ...................................................................................................................................

   ...................................................................................................................................

   5 ...................................................................................................................................

   ................................................................................................... *[5 marks]*

   ii   Design a much improved computer-based data capture form using some of the features described in part **b i** above.

   ...................................................................................................................................

   ...................................................................................................................................

   ...................................................................................................................................

   ...................................................................................................................................

   ...................................................................................................................................

   ...................................................................................................................................

   ...................................................................................................................................

   ...................................................................................................................................

   ...................................................................................................................................

   ...................................................................................................................................

   ................................................................................................... *[4 marks]*

5   The owner of a number of leisure centres has had a new computerised booking system installed.

A systems analyst was brought in to research the existing system and to oversee the installation of the new system.

a   In the table below, tick (✔) the relevant stage of the systems analysis for each of the five named activities:

| Activity | Analysis stage | Design stage | Evaluation stage |
|---|---|---|---|
| Interviewing users of the existing system | | | |
| Planning the validation and verification routines/rules | | | |
| Deciding on the required file structures | | | |
| Interviewing users of the new system | | | |
| Examining existing documentation used in the booking system | | | |

[5 marks]

b   The systems analyst needs to decide the best way to implement the new system. Name and describe **three** different methods of implementation.

Method 1 ..............................................................................................................................................

Description ...........................................................................................................................................

................................................................................................................................................................

................................................................................................................................................................

................................................................................................................................................................

Method 2 ..............................................................................................................................................

Description ...........................................................................................................................................

................................................................................................................................................................

................................................................................................................................................................

................................................................................................................................................................

Method 3 ..............................................................................................................................................

Description ...........................................................................................................................................

................................................................................................................................................................

...........................................................................................................................................................

................................................................................................................................... *[6 marks]*

c   Once the system was fully implemented, the systems analyst handed over documentation to the owner of the leisure centre. The documentation was referred to as: *technical* and *user*.

In the following table indicate, using a tick (✔), which items would be found in the *technical* documentation, in the *user* documentation or in *both* types of documentation.

| Items | Technical | User | Both types |
|---|---|---|---|
| Program listing/coding | | | |
| How to print out data | | | |
| Hardware requirements | | | |
| Software requirements | | | |
| Sample runs (with results) | | | |
| Validation routines | | | |
| Systems flowcharts | | | |
| How to add/delete/amend files | | | |
| Meaning of possible error messages | | | |
| Troubleshooting guide | | | |

*[6 marks]*

6   A system accepts numbers in the range 1 to 50. Tick (✔) whether the following data items are examples of *normal data*, *abnormal data* or *extreme data*.

| Data item | Normal | Abnormal | Extreme |
|---|---|---|---|
| 41 | | | |
| −1 | | | |
| 50 | | | |
| thirty | | | |
| 1 | | | |

*[5 marks]*

7 A new database is being developed for a shop that sells CDs. The new database needs to indicate when stock levels have reached re-order levels. Each CD title needs to be recorded uniquely and the manager also needs to know the last date each CD title was ordered and whether a new order has yet been placed.

a Complete the data dictionary table, giving the full field names to be used in the stock database. It is also necessary to give the *most suitable* validation check to be carried out on each data field and also indicate the data type in each field. (Note: it is not adequate just to say *numeric* for a data type where appropriate.)

| Field name | Validation check | Data type |
|---|---|---|
| cd_title | | alphanumeric |
| | | |
| | | integer |
| last_ordered_date | | |
| | | |

[6 marks]

b Name and describe two methods of **data verification**.

1 ...............................................................................................................................................

.................................................................................................................................................

.................................................................................................................................................

2 ...............................................................................................................................................

.................................................................................................................................................

................................................................................................................... [4 marks]

# (8) Safety and security

1 Use of computers can lead to health and safety risks.

   a Name **three** health risks. For each one, describe what causes the risk and suggest a way of reducing or eliminating the risk.

| Health risk | Description | Elimination |
|---|---|---|
|  |  |  |
|  |  |  |
|  |  |  |

[*9 marks*]

   b Name **two** safety risks. For each one, describe what causes the risk and suggest a way of reducing or eliminating the risk.

| Safety risk | Description | Elimination |
|---|---|---|
|  |  |  |
|  |  |  |

[*6 marks*]

2  a  What is meant by **e-safety**?

......................................................................................................................................................

...................................................................................................................................[1 mark]

   b  Describe **five** ways of ensuring e-safety.

   1  ............................................................................................................................................

      ............................................................................................................................................

      ............................................................................................................................................

   2  ............................................................................................................................................

      ............................................................................................................................................

      ............................................................................................................................................

   3  ............................................................................................................................................

      ............................................................................................................................................

      ............................................................................................................................................

   4  ............................................................................................................................................

      ............................................................................................................................................

      ............................................................................................................................................

   5  ............................................................................................................................................

      ............................................................................................................................................

      ............................................................................................................... [5 marks]

3  Which types of security risks are being described below:

   a  The act of gaining unauthorised access to a computer system with the aim of deleting, changing
      or 'stealing' personal data.

      ............................................................................................................................................

      ............................................................................................................................................

   b  Editing the source code of a program, allowing it to be exploited or changed for a specific purpose;
      it is often done to alter how the software works for a malicious purpose; always an illegal act.

      ............................................................................................................................................

      ............................................................................................................................................

c Software that gathers data by the monitoring of key presses on a user's computer; the gathered data is sent back to the person who sent the malware in the first place.

.................................................................................................................................

.................................................................................................................................

d Program code that can replicate itself with the intention of deleting or corrupting files on a computer.

.................................................................................................................................

.................................................................................................................................

e Junk email sent out to recipients on a mailing list; the emails can clog up bandwidth on the internet and users' in boxes.

.................................................................................................................................

.................................................................................................................................

f An online discussion group in which all the posts are checked by an administrator before they can be posted; this can prevent spam and filter out inappropriate messages and websites.

.................................................................................................................................

.................................................................................................................................

g Small files or code stored on a user's computer sent by a web server; this allows a website to remember a user's preferences each time they visit the website.

.................................................................................................................................

............................................................................................................. *[7 marks]*

4 Explain the following two terms:

a phishing ..........................................................................................................................

.................................................................................................................................

.................................................................................................................................

.................................................................................................................................

b pharming .........................................................................................................................

.................................................................................................................................

.................................................................................................................................

............................................................................................................. *[4 marks]*

5  Indicate (✔) which of the following tasks are carried out by a **firewall**.

| Task | Carried out by a firewall |
|------|---------------------------|
| Firewalls can control employee misconduct or carelessness, preventing them divulging passwords | |
| Firewalls can examine traffic between a user's computer and the public network (e.g. internet) | |
| Firewalls can help to prevent viruses or hackers entering the user's computer or computer network | |
| Firewalls can be used to log all incoming and outgoing traffic to allow later interrogation by a network manager | |
| Firewalls can prevent individuals on internal networks from using their own modems to by-pass the firewall | |
| Firewalls warn the user if software on their computer is trying to access an external data source (e.g. automatic software update) | |

[*4 marks*]

6  a  Explain the following terms:

   i  SSL .............................................................................................................................

   .................................................................................................................................

   .................................................................................................................................

   .................................................................................................................................

   ii  TLS ............................................................................................................................

   .................................................................................................................................

   .................................................................................................................................

   ............................................................................................................... [*5 marks*]


   b  Give **two** differences between SSL and TLS.

   1  .............................................................................................................................

   .................................................................................................................................

   .................................................................................................................................

   .................................................................................................................................

   2  .............................................................................................................................

   .................................................................................................................................

   ............................................................................................................... [*2 marks*] c Five stages that occur when a user wants to access a secure website and receive/send data from/to it are shown below. Put the five stages in their correct order.

1 If the web browser can authenticate the SSL certificate, it sends a message back to the web server to allow communications to begin.

2 The web server responds by sending a copy of its SSL certificate to the user's web browser.

3 The user's web browser sends a message so that it can connect with the required website which is secured by SSL.

4 Once the message is received, the web server acknowledges the web browser and the SSL-encrypted two-way data transfer begins.

5 The web browser requests that the web server identifies itself.

Stages:

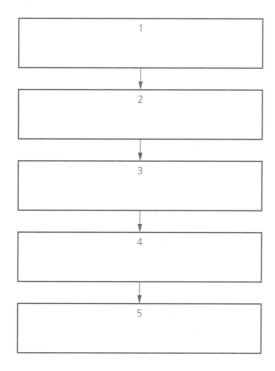

[*5 marks*]

7 a What is meant by **encryption**?

...................................................................................................................................................

...................................................................................................................................................

...................................................................................................................................................

...................................................................................................................................................

...................................................................................................................................................

.......................................................................................................................... [*2 marks*]

b  Complete the diagram by naming the two missing parts A and B.

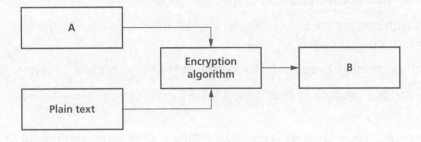

A ...........................................................................................................................................................................

B ............................................................................................................................... [2 marks]

c  If A = 1, E = 2, I = 3, O = 4, U = 5 and Z = A, Y = B, X = C, ... , C = X, B = Y

  i  What message would produce the following encoded message?

     X4NK5G2I HX32MX2 3H U5M

     ...........................................................................................................................................................................

     ...........................................................................................................................................................................

     ...........................................................................................................................................................................

  ii  Encode the following message:

      INFORMATION TECHNOLOGY QUESTION

      ...........................................................................................................................................................................

      ...........................................................................................................................................................................

      ............................................................................................................................... [4 marks]

8  a  What is meant by a **digital certificate**?

      ...........................................................................................................................................................................

      ...........................................................................................................................................................................

      ...............................................................................................................................[1 mark]

b   Name three of the parts that make up a digital certificate.

1   ..........................................................................................................................................

.............................................................................................................................................

.............................................................................................................................................

2   ..........................................................................................................................................

.............................................................................................................................................

.............................................................................................................................................

3   ..........................................................................................................................................

.............................................................................................................................................

................................................................................................................ *[3 marks]*

9   Biometrics is used as a security method in many applications.

Complete the following table which identifies:

- comparative accuracy

- required input devices

- what can interfere with the biometric technique.

| Biometric technique | Comparative accuracy | | Input devices required | What can interfere with biometric technique? |
|---|---|---|---|---|
| | High (✔) | Medium (✔) | | |
| Fingerprinting | | | | |
| Retina scans | | | | |
| Voice recognition | | | | |
| Face recognition | | | | |

*[6 marks]*

10 Discuss the issues of **cloud security**.

.................................................................................................................................................

.................................................................................................................................................

.................................................................................................................................................

.................................................................................................................................................

.................................................................................................................................................

.................................................................................................................................................

.................................................................................................................................................

.................................................................................................................................................

.................................................................................................................................................

.................................................................................................................................................

.................................................................................................................................................

.................................................................................................................................................

.................................................................................................................................................

......................................................................................................................*[6 marks]*

# 9 ) Audiences

1 You are planning and creating a presentation to a group of people.

  a  Give **three** factors which should be considered about the group of people.

    1 ................................................................................................................................

    ................................................................................................................................

    2 ................................................................................................................................

    ................................................................................................................................

    3 ................................................................................................................................

    ................................................................................................. *[3 marks]*

  b  Give **three** methods of finding out information about the target audience.

    1 ................................................................................................................................

    ................................................................................................................................

    2 ................................................................................................................................

    ................................................................................................................................

    3 ................................................................................................................................

    ................................................................................................. *[3 marks]*

2  a  What is meant by **software piracy**?

    ................................................................................................................................

    .................................................................................................... *[1 mark]*

  b  Describe **three** methods to protect software from piracy.

    1 ................................................................................................................................

    ................................................................................................................................

    2 ................................................................................................................................

    ................................................................................................................................

    3 ................................................................................................................................

    ................................................................................................. *[3 marks]*

3 The five items shown need to be considered when giving a presentation.

For each item, give **one** example of what needs to be considered.

a Language used ............................................................................................................................

b Multimedia used .......................................................................................................................

c Length of presentation............................................................................................................

d Interactive presentation .........................................................................................................

e Examples to be used ...................................................................................................... [5 marks]

4 Four terms and four descriptions are shown in the diagram. By drawing arrows, connect each term to its correct description.

| | |
|---|---|
| Legal | This refers to attitudes, values and practices shared by a society or group of people |
| Morality | This covers the law, whether a person's action is punishable by law |
| Ethics | This governs professional interactions, codes of behaviour practised by a society or group of people |
| Culture | This governs the private and personal interactions between people and is usually determined by the person concerned |

[4 marks]

5 During the day, Sergey works in a company that develops software for the nuclear industry. He works with a team of programmers.

In the evening he works for himself writing games software. He frequently hires the services of other programmers to speed up the process of developing his games software,

The table shows a number of statements about Sergey's activities. By ticking (✔) one or more columns indicate whether each statement is an example of **unethical, immoral** or **illegal** activity.

| Statement | Unethical | Immoral | Illegal |
|---|---|---|---|
| Sergey uses some of the software routines from his day job when writing his games software | | | |
| Sergey claims that all the software routines he uses from his day job were written by himself | | | |
| Sergey has some of his software written overseas, but only pays the writers a very low wage | | | |

| | | | |
|---|---|---|---|
| Sergey writes some of his computer games using the powerful computer systems available to him during his day job | | | |
| To help advertise his games, Sergey hires a 'hacker' who breaks into websites so that **popups** appear which advertise his games free of charge | | | |
| Some of the games software written by Sergey make fun of people who have certain disabilities | | | |
| Some of the games Sergey writes collect information from the user's computer, where it is installed. This data is sent back to Sergey for various uses | | | |

[*7 marks*]

# (10) Communication

1 a  Most countries in the world have laws governing email content.

Give **three** examples of these laws.

1 .................................................................................................................................

..................................................................................................................................

..................................................................................................................................

2 .................................................................................................................................

..................................................................................................................................

..................................................................................................................................

3 .................................................................................................................................

..................................................................................................................................

.................................................................................................. *[3 marks]*

b  Explain the difference between **passive** and **active** attacks by email.

..................................................................................................................................

..................................................................................................................................

..................................................................................................................................

..................................................................................................................................

..................................................................................................................................

.................................................................................................. *[3 marks]*

c  Give **three** reasons why users set up **email groups**.

1 .................................................................................................................................

..................................................................................................................................

..................................................................................................................................

2 .................................................................................................................................

..................................................................................................................................

..................................................................................................................................

3 .................................................................................................................................

..................................................................................................................................

...................................................................................................*[3 marks]*

  Photocopying prohibited

2  a  The internet and intranets are two different types of network.

Tick (✔) the appropriate columns to show which features refer to the internet and which features refer to intranets.

| Feature | Internet | Intranets |
|---|---|---|
| Information available to users is specific to a particular company or organisation only | | |
| Requires passwords and user ids to be entered to gain access to the network | | |
| Allows public access to information on a global scale | | |
| Sits behind a firewall to give protection from hackers and from viruses | | |
| By using an ISP account it is possible to access the network from anywhere in the world | | |

[5 marks]

b  The following diagram shows an **extranet**.

Complete the diagram by naming parts **A**, **B** and **C**.

Internal company network (intranet)

A = ........................................................

.............................................................

B = ........................................................

.............................................................

C = ........................................................

.............................................................

[3 marks]

c  Give **three** advantages of using intranets rather than the internet.

1  ...........................................................................................................................

...........................................................................................................................

...........................................................................................................................

2  ...........................................................................................................................

...........................................................................................................................

........................................................................................................... [3 marks]

3  ...........................................................................................................................

...........................................................................................................................

...........................................................................................................................

3 a Which type of **cloud storage** is being described below:

   i   A storage environment where customer/client and cloud storage provider are different companies.

   .................................................................................................................................

   ii  Storage provided by a dedicated environment behind a company firewall; customer/ client and cloud storage provider are integrated and operate as a single entity.

   .................................................................................................................................

   iii Some of the data resides behind an integrated cloud storage facility while less sensitive data can be accessed from a separate and different cloud storage provider.

   ............................................................................................................. [3 marks]

   b  Give **two** advantages and **two** disadvantages of using cloud storage.

      Advantages

      1  ............................................................................................................................

         ............................................................................................................................

      2  ............................................................................................................................

         ............................................................................................................................

      Disadvantages

      1  ............................................................................................................................

         ............................................................................................................................

      2  ............................................................................................................................

         ..................................................................................................... [4 marks]

4 a Explain how you would know if a website has security authentication or encryption.

   .................................................................................................................................

   .................................................................................................................................

   ..................................................................................................................... [1 mark]

Photocopying prohibited

b In each of the following tick (✔) the appropriate box to indicate the correct meaning of the given term.

i Meaning of **http.**

| Meaning | (✔) |
|---|---|
| hypertext transfer program | |
| hypertext transfer protocol | |
| hybrid text transaction protocol | |
| handshaking text transfer protocol | |

ii Meaning of **ftp.**

| Meaning | (✔) |
|---|---|
| fixed type protocol | |
| format testing profile | |
| faster transfer protocol | |
| file transfer protocol | |

iii Meaning of **pdf.**

| Meaning | (✔) |
|---|---|
| protected document format | |
| portable document format | |
| principal document format | |
| portable document file | |

iv  Meaning of **url**.

| Meaning | (✔) |
|---|---|
| uploading remote language | |
| user router locator | |
| uniform resource locator | |
| uniform remote linker | |

[*4 marks*]

c  Describe **three** features found in most web browsers.

1 ...................................................................................................................................

...................................................................................................................................

...................................................................................................................................

2 ...................................................................................................................................

...................................................................................................................................

...................................................................................................................................

3 ...................................................................................................................................

...................................................................................................................................

................................................................................................................... [*3 marks*]

d  A user typed in:

http://www.hoddereducation.co.uk/ICT_books/2017

Identify the three different internet components shown in the above url.

1 ...................................................................................................................................

...................................................................................................................................

2 ...................................................................................................................................

...................................................................................................................................

3 ...................................................................................................................................

................................................................................................................... [*3 marks*]

Photocopying prohibited

5 Explain the main differences between **ftp** and **http**.

.........................................................................................................................................................

.........................................................................................................................................................

.........................................................................................................................................................

.........................................................................................................................................................

.........................................................................................................................................................

.........................................................................................................................................................

.........................................................................................................................................................

.........................................................................................................................................................

................................................................................................................................... [4 marks]

6  a  The following table shows features of blogs and wikis. Tick (✔) the appropriate columns to show which are features of blogs and which are features of wikis.

| Feature | Blogs | Wikis |
|---|---|---|
| Updated on a regular basis by the author only | | |
| Anyone can edit, delete or modify the content | | |
| Organised in reverse chronological order | | |
| Can only be updated and edited by the author | | |
| Can be easily edited using a web browser | | |

[5 marks]

b  Give **four** features of a typical **social networking site**.

1  ...............................................................................................................................................

...............................................................................................................................................

2  ...............................................................................................................................................

...............................................................................................................................................

3  ...............................................................................................................................................

...............................................................................................................................................

4  ...............................................................................................................................................

................................................................................................................................... [4 marks]

c Explain the meaning of the following terms:

i ISP ................................................................................................................................

...................................................................................................................................

...................................................................................................................................

ii netiquette .....................................................................................................................

...................................................................................................................................

...................................................................................................................................

iii virtual private network (VPN) .......................................................................................

...................................................................................................................................

...................................................................................................................................

iv microblog

...................................................................................................................................

.................................................................................................................... [6 marks]

7 Describe **three** advantages and **three** disadvantages of using **search engines** to research for information.

Advantages

1 .....................................................................................................................................

...................................................................................................................................

2 .....................................................................................................................................

...................................................................................................................................

3 .....................................................................................................................................

...................................................................................................................................

Disadvantages

1 .....................................................................................................................................

...................................................................................................................................

2 .....................................................................................................................................

...................................................................................................................................

3 .....................................................................................................................................

.................................................................................................................... [6 marks]

8  Discuss how you would evaluate the reliability of information found on the internet.

.................................................................................................................................................................

.................................................................................................................................................................

.................................................................................................................................................................

.................................................................................................................................................................

.................................................................................................................................................................

.................................................................................................................................................................

.................................................................................................................................................................

.................................................................................................................................................................

.................................................................................................................................................................

.................................................................................................................................................................

.................................................................................................................................................................

.................................................................................................................................................................

.................................................................................................................................................................

.................................................................................................................................................................

.................................................................................................................................................................

................................................................................................................... *[7 marks]*

# Cambridge IGCSE™
# ICT Theory

Workbook

This workbook supports students using the Cambridge IGCSE™ ICT textbook, providing plenty of extra practice questions and activities for the theory paper.

- Perfect for using throughout the course – ensures students learn each topic thoroughly
- Focuses on the Theory section of the syllabus
- Answers are available online

Working for over **25 YEARS** WITH Cambridge Assessment International Education

For over 25 years we have been trusted by Cambridge schools around the world to provide quality support for teaching and learning. For this reason we have been selected by Cambridge Assessment International Education as an official publisher of endorsed material for their syllabuses.

ISBN 978-1-471-89036-9

9 781471 890369

**HODDER EDUCATION**

www.hoddereducation.com